WRITE LIKE

WRITING TO INFORM

FRANCES K. HUBBARD and LAUREN SPENCER

rosen publishing's
rosen central®

New York

Published in 2012 by The Rosen Publishing Group, Inc.
29 East 21st Street, New York, NY 10010

Library of Congress Cataloging-in-Publication Data

Hubbard, Frances K.
Writing to inform/Frances K. Hubbard, Lauren Spencer.—1st ed.
        p. cm.—(Write like a pro)
Includes bibliographical references and index.
ISBN 978-1-4488-4681-8 (library binding)—ISBN 978-1-4488-4687-0
(pbk.)—ISBN 978-1-4488-4745-7 (6-pack)
1. Composition (Language arts)—Juvenile literature. 2. English language—
Paragraphs—Juvenile literature. I. Spencer, Lauren. II. Title.
LB1576.H697 2012
372.62'3044—dc22

                                                                    2011006535

Manufactured in the United States of America

CPSIA Compliance Information: Batch #S11YA: For further information, contact Rosen Publishing, New York, New York, at 1-800-237-9932.

CONTENTS

INTRODUCTION

Biographies, classroom essays, reports, and expository pieces are all types of informative writing. A personal essay or post on a blog can be considered informative when it focuses only on the facts surrounding an experience. The goal of this style of writing is to present clear information about a specific topic. Informative writing is objective, meaning that it deals with only the facts surrounding a subject. The facts that are provided in informative writing should be balanced and well researched.

Some teachers will ask you to get up in front of the class and read your work to the rest of the students. This can help you determine where your writing may need some work.

You, as the author, have the chance to take one topic and explore it in detail so that your audience will be more informed. This process can be fun, since it will give you the opportunity to zero in on one subject and find out everything there is to know about it. Since informative writing requires you to be very clear about the facts you find to support your topic, you can become an authority through the research that you do.

In this book, we will investigate the many styles of informative writing. We will examine how to focus closely on a topic so that you can gather and organize facts and begin the writing process.

We will also focus on new methods of gathering information, such as conducting a personal interview. We will discover ways to keep track of information sources in order to maintain an organized system of research. Finally, we will look at how computers and the Internet play an important role in informative writing.

Once your article is completed, you will then have a chance to polish it and present it to an audience. Although the goal of any informative writing is to organize a story in a straightforward manner, it can still be written with style and personality. In this book, we will discover various methods of using creative writing elements to enhance your writing skills. In the end, your author's voice will resound loudly while your readers gain clear insight into your chosen topic.

chapter 1

Preparing to Write

When you write an informative story, your goal is to find the best way to deliver facts about a specific subject. You are not trying to persuade your reader to take a certain point of view. You are instead supplying your reader with objective facts, rather than subjective opinions. A fact can be proven true; therefore, it is objective. An opinion involves your personal feelings about something, therefore it is subjective.

When you write an informational piece, you should note only the facts about your subject. This type of writing depends on well-researched information to support it. Various types of styles can categorize informative writing.

ESSENTIAL STEPS

Begin to familiarize yourself with different types of informative writing styles.

Search for a focus for your informative piece.

What Is Expository Writing?

Expository writing is designed to explain a topic. It often gives facts, explains ideas, or defines conditions. Whether it's giving directions or explaining how to accomplish something, an expository piece is helpful because it provides the reader with deeper insight into a subject. With this type of informative writing, ideas are presented in a certain order so that the reader can follow the explanation easily. When deciding upon a topic for an expository piece, choose one that you feel can be clearly and simply explained. If your topic requires diagrams, such as in a visual how-to manual, then the subject matter is probably too complicated to be described using only words. For instance, choosing a topic like "How to Make a Movie" would be too broad, but explaining "How to Make a Short Film in Your Own Backyard" could work more easily.

To draw the reader into the piece, include details that grab attention. Engage your audience by detailing where to find basic props, the best times of day to film, and how to edit the film and upload it to the Internet. Recounting your own experience with this subject by using the five senses (sight, sound, smell, taste, and touch) can enhance the writing and add a human touch. This will prevent your piece from becoming strictly a "how-to" list.

What Is Biographical Writing?

In biographical writing, your goal is to communicate information about the events in a specific person's life. In a biography, the story normally flows in a chronological order with one event following another. This information may start at the point when and where the subject was born and explain how he or she lived, but it might also

Actor Daniel Radcliffe first gained international fame when he took the role of Harry Potter in the popular movie franchise. He also makes an interesting subject for an informative paper.

begin during a more specific time in the subject's life. For instance, if the actor Daniel Radcliffe is your subject, then you need to decide what specific period in his life you'd like to write about. Depending on the length of your paper, you could cover many angles of Radcliffe's life and career in an organized manner. Using the five W's (who, what, where, when, and why) and the two H's (how and how much) as your foundation, you will achieve a strong base on which to build your story.

What Are Essays and Reports?

An informational essay investigates a topic by exploring it fully from all sides. An informative essay can be about a personal subject as long as you present only the facts. For instance, if you choose to write about a video camera, you would include factual details such as what kind it is, when you got it, and where you use it. Again, the five W's and two H's will serve as a solid

DIFFERENT ESSAY TYPES

Many essays offer opposing viewpoints, which present arguments in two parts. One common type of essay is called the comparison and contrast essay. Other essays are similar to the comparison and contrast essay, though they might be referred to as the cause and effect essay, the problem and solution essay, or the before and after essay.

HARRISCOUNTY
PUBLIC**LIBRARY**
your pathway to knowledge

PROGRAM FOR ADULTS !

MAKE YOUR OWN NATURAL DOG BISCUITS

Thursday, June 8 - 4:30pm

Katherine Tyra Library
16719 Clay Rd.
Houston, TX 77084
281-550-0885

Programs and services are Americans with Disabilities Act (ADA) Compliant. Special accommodations can be requested in advance by contacting the library.

Come to this special adult summer program to make your own dog biscuits! This healthy treat for pets is easy to make. Make some for your own dog, or give some away as a gift! Supplies & ingredients provided.

basis for what details to include. By asking yourself who, what, when, where, why, how, and how much, you can be secure in the knowledge that your facts are well presented. Next, you'll want to add details to those facts.

A report is a much more in-depth investigation of a topic. Informational reports require a solid, well-researched foundation to support the subject. An informational report about your video camera could even cover the history of your particular make and model. This likely means that you'll be reading about your subject before organizing the facts you've learned into a solid story.

Picking a Subject

If your topic is too broad, you will need to refine it. A graphic organizer could help you pinpoint a more specific subject on which to focus. The easiest way to do this is to find a graphic organizer template on the Internet. You can download the template and even print it or just draw one yourself. One good type of graphic organizer is a web diagram (see page 12). Inside the center circle, write your broad topic, "Movies" (see example). Around the main circle are additional circles that branch off from the main one. In these circles, write more specific subjects like

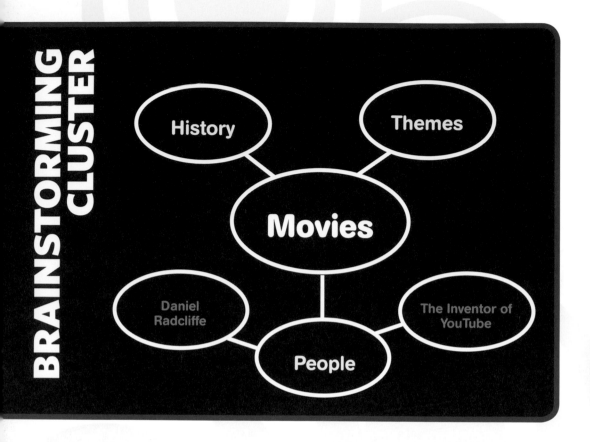

BRAINSTORMING CLUSTER

"People," "History," and "Themes." From there you can extend more lines and circles from these topics and write in very specific topics, such as "Daniel Radcliffe" and "The Inventor of YouTube" coming from "People," and so on until all the circles are filled.

Once it is complete, examine your diagram and choose the topic that interests you most. The topic you choose should offer you the opportunity to inform your readers by writing about well-researched facts. The writing process (prewriting, first draft, revising, editing, final draft) will help you enhance those facts with interesting details.

Writing the Facts

Write about the following topics objectively (writing only facts), using each informative style:

- Expository: Ten steps to finding a birthday present for your best friend.
- Biography: A day in the life of your favorite pop singer.
- Essay: Your best day.
- Report: A cause that you strongly believe in.

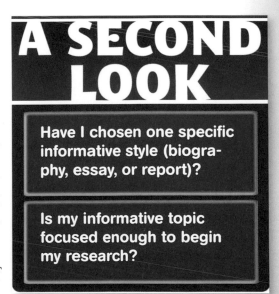

A SECOND LOOK

Have I chosen one specific informative style (biography, essay, or report)?

Is my informative topic focused enough to begin my research?

Now that you have practiced writing objectively about familiar situations, you should begin by researching your chosen topic for your first draft. There are many methods of conducting research in a thorough manner. If you have chosen to write a biography, for example, you'll want to observe the person firsthand. If that isn't possible, try to read interviews with him or her, or books related to his or her life. Start thinking like a private detective and investigate your subject. Writing a clear sentence that defines your subject might help you zoom in and focus on your topic. Making a list that describes your subject may also help you gain insight. Keep in mind that your ultimate goal in informative writing is to explain facts about your subject to the reader.

chapter 2

Research and Getting Organized

Because informative stories depend on facts, research is a crucial element in laying their foundation. There are many ways to find the information you will need to develop your story.

First, think about what you need to learn in order to deliver the most important facts about your topic. Then determine what you need to learn in order to make your information even better. A KWL (Know, Want to Know, Learned) chart will come in handy for this process.

Write your topic at the top of a blank sheet of paper. Next, make three columns. Above the first column write the heading "What Do I Know?" Then, make a list of those things underneath the first heading. In the second column, under the heading "What Do I Want to Know?" complete another

ESSENTIAL STEPS

Gather all the information for your topic.

Organize your information for easy access.

list. Write down everything that comes to mind. Remember that this column will be longer than the first one. The answers to these questions will become the "wheels" that keep your story rolling. Your third column has the heading "What Have I Learned?" and will remain blank for now. As you figure out the answers to your questions, you can return to fill in the third column.

If you decide to write about your family or friends, you can go through old photo albums to help generate some good ideas.

Finding the Right Information

Whether you are focusing on expository, biographical, essay, or report writing, you'll want to determine where you can obtain the facts needed to support your topic. Books and the Internet are both great resources, as are the people around you, especially if you are writing about someone in your own life.

Grab a pencil and paper and ask questions about your subject. Observe him or her, carefully writing down details about his or her appearance, mannerisms, habits, actions, and lifestyle. Make sure the person knows that you are doing this research, so that he or she feels comfortable enough to help you. You can also utilize journals and photo albums to help remind you of specific incidents. Examining these experiences will help you determine interesting supporting details later.

If you are writing a biography of someone you know and he or she is available, request an interview. Prepare for the meeting by writing questions ahead of time. Also, while you're conducting the interview, follow the conversation wherever it takes you. If he or she answers one of your questions with information that makes you curious about something else, ask about it. Sometimes this freestyle interviewing takes practice. If you don't feel confident enough to have the subject lead the conversation, gently guide him or her back to your list of questions. Before you close the interview, examine your notes to be certain that you've gotten all the information you expected.

Anecdotes, which are interesting little stories that have to do with the subject, are a great way to add personality to writing. Most people enjoy discovering little-known facts about a person's life or a certain topic. Anecdotal material often has the effect of

Biography of Daniel Radcliffe

What do I know?	What do I want to know?	What have I learned?
He's the star of the *Harry Potter* movies.	How did he get the part?	
He lives in England.	Where was he born and raised?	
He is involved in charity work.	What inspired him to get involved?	
	What is his proudest moment as an actor?	
	What's the scariest thing that's ever happened during a shoot?	

getting people's attention because it's like sharing a secret. Readers feel as if they've gotten a piece of information that is special. The way to find anecdotal material is to use sources that are off the regular research track. Instead of relying only on an encyclopedia's condensed summary about a person's life or an event, try to find a book that will give you more detailed background information about your subject. Once you locate a comprehensive resource, you're bound to come across interesting facts and anecdotal information to include in your story.

Plagiarism

Avoid directly copying word for word any research material you've come across in books, in magazines, on the Internet, or through any published sources. This way you will avoid charges of plagiarism, which is a very serious matter. The definition of plagiarism, according to *Webster's New World Dictionary*, is "to take ideas, writing, etc. from another and pass them off as one's own." This definition is in quotes because it was copied from the dictionary. If you are required to use a passage word for word, keep it brief, use quotation marks around the actual words, and be sure to give the author credit by mentioning where you found his or her work. If you want to use it without a direct quotation, then you must paraphrase it. Paraphrasing means to change the actual words in a written passage while keeping the meaning similar.

Tracking Your Research

It's helpful to keep an organized list of where you found the information you are using for your story. You can either add these notes to the "Learned" column of your KWL chart, or for more extensive research, assemble a "gathering grid." Its purpose is to map out where you found certain information so that if you need to add more details or want to check your facts, you'll know exactly where to return to find it. Take the "Want to Know" questions from your KWL chart and write them down the left side of a blank piece of paper. Then, along the top of the page, note the places where you're finding the answers. These are called sources. Next, fill in the information as you come across it.

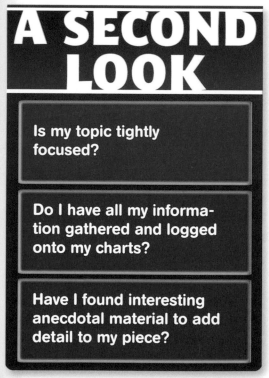

A SECOND LOOK

Is my topic tightly focused?

Do I have all my information gathered and logged onto my charts?

Have I found interesting anecdotal material to add detail to my piece?

Learning how to research a person or a topic is essential to effective writing. Understanding how to use the Internet, where to go for reliable facts,

Gathering Grid

Subject: Daniel Radcliffe	His biography, *No Ordinary Wizard*	Internet www .danradcliffe .com	*US Weekly*
Where was he born?	Fulham, a suburb of London		
How did he become an actor?		He auditioned for a part in *David Copperfield*	
How did he land the role of Harry Potter?		He caught the eye of director Chris Columbus and producer David Heyman	
Does he want to do another *Harry Potter* movie?			No, he would like to move on to some new projects.
When was he born?		Born July 23, 1989	

and how to use unconventional methods of discovery will all help you create interesting, informative pieces. Remember, while it's easy to become overwhelmed when conducting research for any topic, focusing only on your subject and staying organized will serve you well throughout this process.

chapter 3
Your First Draft

The first step to beginning any informative writing is organizing your research. Informative pieces use a solid story structure based on researched facts to weave everything together. The beginning introduces your topic sentence and grabs the reader's attention, the middle unveils supporting details and anecdotes about your topic, and the end wraps up the overall story by reinforcing the original point. Many times, this conclusion will reiterate the same point as your topic sentence. The movement of your piece is like a circle because the conclusion will bring you right back to the start.

An outline is a very helpful tool to organize any writing piece. Outlines help writers distribute their research by prioritizing and rearranging it to form a logical beginning, middle, and end. Constructing

ESSENTIAL STEPS

Organize your research.

Focus on the structure (beginning, middle, end) of the piece.

Begin writing.

an outline will give you a chance to see the "shape" of your story. Using an outline will also help you to set up your topic in an accessible way so that you can sail into the writing with no interruptions. Here is an example of an outline for a multiparagraphed essay:

Working Title: "Excellent Moments"

I. Introduction (Beginning Paragraph)

    A. This is where you write your topic sentence: "I am the luckiest kid on earth."

    B. Focus on the main points that will be covered in the piece:

        1. Activities at home

        2. Activities at school

        3. Activities in sports

II. Supporting Paragraph (Point 1)

Transition sentence about home: "I wake up in my clean room!" (Use descriptive details that paint a mental picture.)

        1. Finishing my chores and earning my allowance.

        2. Recounting the story of the basketball hoop I built with my dad in the backyard.

III. Supporting Paragraph (Point 2)

A. Transition sentence about school: "When I get to school, I walk down the hallway and see the essay that I wrote hanging on the wall."

B. Use descriptive details that paint a mental picture:
   1. Awards I've won
   2. Friends I've made

IV. Supporting Paragraph (Point 3)

A. Transition sentence about sports: "After school on Mondays, Wednesdays, and Fridays I go to the baseball field behind my school."

B. Use descriptive details that paint a mental picture:
   1. Baseball
   2. Swimming coach at camp

V. Conclusion/End Paragraph

Review your points and express a last thought or feeling on the topic to bring it all together:
   1. Home
   2. School
   3. Sports

Your Writing Tools

Now that you're ready to start writing, find a place where you won't be interrupted. Gather your research, outline, and other writing tools. Focus first on your topic sentence, which explains the main idea that your informative story will revolve around. Begin by concentrating on this main topic. Keep the topic sentence simple, enlightening, and interesting. This first paragraph is a preview of the information that lies ahead.

Your notebook is one of the most important tools you can have as a writer. You can take notes in it or even begin to write and revise.

As you continue writing, let your author's "voice" shine. Your author's voice is the individual style that you use in your writing that gives it personality. Your voice establishes the story's tone and sets it apart from other writing by using interesting details and rich descriptions. You may have heard the saying, "Write like you speak." This can be true even in an informative piece that relies heavily on facts. By eliminating the awkwardness of everyday speech (all of the "uhs" and "likes" for instance), you can establish a tone that helps the reader connect to you. Once you reach the story's conclusion, close it by reinforcing the main point. See the example below.

Document1

Excellent Moments

I am the luckiest kid on earth. I work hard at home, in school, and on various sports teams. From the time I wake up in the morning to the time I go to sleep at night, I am usually happy and enthusiastic.

I wake up in the morning in my clean room. Every week I make sure my bedroom is organized so that I can earn my allowance and find everything I need. From the window of my room, I can see the basketball hoop my dad and I built last summer.

When I get to school, I walk down the hallway and see an essay that I wrote hanging on the wall. That makes me proud. I always get together with my good friends Sean and Evelyn before we go to class. We work hard to do well.

After school on Mondays, Wednesdays, and Fridays, I go to the baseball field behind my school. The name of our team is the Red Caps. During the summer, I help the swimming coach at camp.

Page 1   Sec 1   1/1   At 1"   Ln 1   Col 1   0/0   ○REC ○TRK ○EXT ○OVR

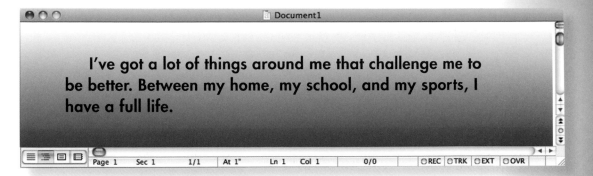

I've got a lot of things around me that challenge me to be better. Between my home, my school, and my sports, I have a full life.

The personal essay above includes important information about the author's feelings of luck. He supports his topic in an orderly way, following the outline. The introductory paragraph establishes the topic, while each supporting paragraph covers only one point using facts, descriptive adjectives, and anecdotes (like the building of the basketball hoop) to draw the reader into the writer's world and get across the main message. The concluding paragraph wraps it all up with a review of what's been covered along with a final comment regarding the main point.

Following is another example of a first draft. This one is a report that uses a rhetorical question as its topic sentence.

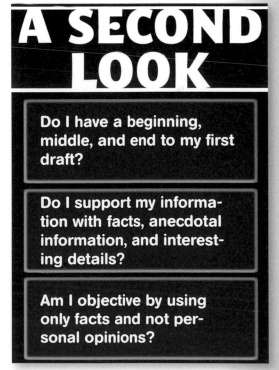

A SECOND LOOK

Do I have a beginning, middle, and end to my first draft?

Do I support my information with facts, anecdotal information, and interesting details?

Am I objective by using only facts and not personal opinions?

Document1

The Cult of Death

Can you imagine a culture so obsessed with the afterlife that its people spent a majority of their life preparing for death? Just such a culture was that of ancient Egypt. In fact, many Egyptians devoted their lives to the building of tombs to house Egyptian kings, known as pharaohs.

Proof of the importance that Egyptians attached to death can be seen in their rituals. One of the most well-known ancient Egyptian rituals is the process of mummification. The bodies of many ancient Egyptians, not only pharaohs, were preserved in the earth as mummies. Mummification originated in Egypt, where its people were naturally preserved in dry sands. The process of Egyptian mummification was elaborate. It relied on a special ingredient called natron, a salt that dehydrated human tissue. Taking out internal organs and filling the corpse with herbs helped speed the drying.

The Book of the Dead, a collection of ancient Egyptian texts, is historical proof of the importance Egyptians placed on preparing for death. It is a collection of spells related to the afterlife. It was commonly placed in the tomb with the deceased, who was meant to read it during the journey to the next world.

As you can tell, death was important to the ancient Egyptians. The remains of their art, writing, tombs, and mummified bodies are proof of the importance they attached to the afterlife. Today these artifacts remain to tell the tale of life in ancient Egypt.

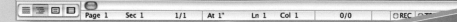

Page 1   Sec 1   1/1   At 1"   Ln 1   Col 1   0/0   ○REC

Finally, reread your draft. At this point, you can decide if you need to do additional research to support your topic. If so, mark up the draft, noting all the places where you need additional information to reinforce your main ideas. If not, you can move on to the next phase of writing. In the next chapter, we will discuss other methods of revising your draft.

Rhetorical Questions

Rhetorical questions focus attention directly on the reader by asking him or her to respond to something that has to do with the informative subject. Rhetorical questions can sometimes be used in an opening sentence to introduce the topic

Example: Have you ever wondered why it's so difficult to find the perfect pair of sneakers?

At this point, your reader will respond. Now you can continue your writing to inform him or her of useful ways in which to locate appropriate footwear.

chapter 4

Making Revisions

As an author, revising any piece of writing is a crucial step in the process. The act of revising is more than improving spelling and punctuation, which is a step that will come later. Revising is achieved by looking beyond the surface of your writing to find sections to expand or to clarify information. Whenever you revise your writing, you should edit your work line by line, ensuring that your sentences are meaningful, logical, and concise.

With your first draft in front of you, make sure you've got your gathering grid and KWL chart handy so you can insert into your draft any researched material that you may have left out. Again, reread your first draft. Make notations in the margins where information needs to be added. This process will help you focus on areas that need improvement. Look for places where you can add descriptive

ESSENTIAL STEPS

Refine or add facts and details to your piece.

Make sure details paint a vivid mental picture.

Work on transitions and sentence structure.

details to your story. This process of reexamination will help polish your distinctive author's voice.

What Are Transitions?

Shifting smoothly from one thought to the next in a written work is important. As an author, your role is to share details about your topic in such a way that your reader has gotten everything that he or she needs without feeling that the ride was too bumpy. Transitions are the key to a smooth journey. They join ideas about your subject together from sentence to sentence, and paragraph to paragraph.

If you are writing a biographical or expository story, then your transitions may follow a chronological order. Avoid overusing "and then" at the beginning of sentences and instead employ a variety of words to connect your thoughts. For essays and reports, your informative style may be more fluid, although transitions are still the key to maintaining the momentum. Examine the chart on the following page for ideas.

What Is Sentence Structure?

Part of the revision process depends on reviewing the types of sentences you have written. Weak writing is sometimes the result of poor sentence structure and redundancy. If all of your sentences are a similar length and are structured in the same way, then your writing may bore the reader. He or she can quickly lose interest. In the following section, we will briefly define various types of sentences. As a writer, you should strive to use a variety of sentence types and lengths.

TRANSITIONAL WORDS: To Add Information

Again	And	Besides	Finally
Along with	Another	For example	In addition
Also	As well	For instance	Next

TRANSITIONAL WORDS: Location

Above	Around	Between	Inside	Outside
Across	Behind	By	Into	Over
Against	Below	Down	Near	Throughout
Along	Beneath	In back of	Off	To the right/ left
Among	Beside	In front of	On top of	Under

TRANSITIONAL WORDS: Time

About	Before	Later	Soon	Tomorrow
After	During	Meanwhile	Then	Until
As soon as	Finally	Next	Third	When
At	First	Second	Today	Yesterday

TRANSITIONAL WORDS: Conclusion or Summary

As a result	Lastly	In summary
Finally	In conclusion	Therefore

Declarative Sentences

A declarative sentence makes a strong statement. It announces something without trying to persuade. A declarative sentence tells a fact about a person, place, or thing in a forceful, clear, and concise manner. Example:

> **In order to find the perfect sneaker, you need to know your shoe size.**

Compound Sentences

A compound sentence links two simple sentences, or independent clauses. When you join together two complete sentences containing a subject and a verb, you create a compound sentence. This can be achieved by using a semicolon or a conjunction ("and," or," and "but"). Examples:

> **Sporting goods stores carry a large selection of sneakers in many colors and sizes; you need to know your shoe size in order to find a pair that will fit you.**

Or use a conjunction:

> **Sporting goods stores carry a large selection of sneakers in many colors and sizes, but you need to know your shoe size in order to find a pair that will fit you.**

Complex Sentences

Putting a dependent clause—so-called because it can't exist alone—into a complete sentence makes it a complex sentence. Example:

> **The sporting goods store, which has a huge selection of colors and sizes of sneakers, is filled with salespeople eager to help customers.**

Add (or Keep As Is) +
- Sentences that connect to your main topic or point
- Sentences that use interesting, important, and entertaining facts
- Sentences that support the subject with details and examples

Subtract (or Rewrite) –
- A topic sentence or a paragraph that is confusing or dull
- Sentences that are crowded with extra facts that don't reinforce your topic
- Sentences that do not include detail or are not focused

While the sentence "The sporting goods store is filled with salespeople eager to help customers" is complete on its own, adding "which has a huge selection of colors and sizes of sneakers" provides a valuable detail. When revising any work, part of the process is to ensure that you have used verbs correctly. In most cases, the verb tense should be consistent throughout your informative piece. Verbs can be written in the present, past, or future tense (see examples, page 40). If your piece takes place in the present tense, for example, then all sentences should be written in the present tense.

Making Sure That Your Revision Is Thorough

In informative writing, it's important to always remember the main point. Check the "add or subtract chart" on the facing page to make sure important revisions have occurred.

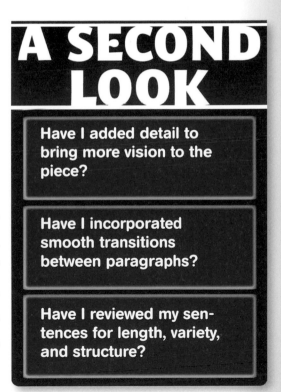

A SECOND LOOK

Have I added detail to bring more vision to the piece?

Have I incorporated smooth transitions between paragraphs?

Have I reviewed my sentences for length, variety, and structure?

Authors normally revise their work several times. There are many ways to improve your writing at this stage. In addition to the ones we've mentioned in this chapter (varying sentence structure, watching verb tense agreement, and writing transitions), many authors rewrite for clarity or edit their work for overall content and length.

Consult a thesaurus and consider replacing adjectives and adverbs with others that are closer in meaning to what you wanted to say. If you feel that your piece is lacking in detail, consider doing additional research. Make sure that your pronouns agree with their antecedents, or the noun that the pronoun is replacing. For instance, it is incorrect to write, "A reader might enjoy stories about their family." The correct version of this statement should read, "A reader might enjoy stories about his or her family." Watch out for run-on sentences, which occur when two or more simple sentences are joined without a conjunction or punctuation. Beware also of sentence fragments, which often do not contain a complete subject and verb.

chapter 5
Editing and Proofreading

Until now, you've probably been using a temporary title (often referred to as a "working" title). Because this is the "flag" that sets your story in motion, it carries a lot of responsibility. The title needs to grab the reader's attention. Think of the title as a way to tease readers, or give them just enough information to make them want to learn more about your subject. Read through your informative story and look for a descriptive word or phrase that will breathe life into your title. While "The History of Gaming" is basic and informative, it's too bland.

Instead, think of a title that relies on the element of mystery, such as "The Top Secret World of Gaming," or one that tempts the reader, such as "The Triumphs and Tribulations of Video Gaming." You can

ESSENTIAL STEPS

Add your title.

Complete spelling, grammar, and fact-checking.

Ask others for feedback.

Finish the final draft.

also use a subtitle, which is an explanatory phrase that supports the main title. For example: "Gaming: An Insider's Look." If you have several titles that you like, ask a partner or the class if they can help you choose one. Also, make sure that your name appears near the title or at the end of your piece.

Before sharing your informative writing with anyone for a final edit, so that he or she will look it over for weaknesses, it's important to spend some time checking for any spelling and grammar problems. If you've typed the story into a computer, use spelling and grammar check to correct any mistakes. If your piece is handwritten, use a different-colored pen to circle any words that you think are misspelled. Have your dictionary handy and look up everything you've circled, making corrections directly on the page. Grammar and punctuation are also important elements to double-check.

Avoiding Word Confusion

The spelling of certain words causes great confusion. Sometimes this bewilderment has to do with possessive words, which are words that show ownership, versus contractions, which join two words together using an apostrophe (see example chart, page 39).

Homophones can also cause confusion. A homophone is a word that has the same sound as another word but a completely different meaning. Some examples of homophones are "affect" and "effect"; "bear" and "bare"; "blew" and "blue"; and "cent," "scent," and "sent." Check a dictionary if you have any questions about a word's meaning.

Possessive (shows ownership)	Contraction (joins two words together)
Their Their video game system is kept in the den. ("Their" shows possession/ownership of the video game system.)	**They're** They're playing after school. ("They're" is short for "They are.")
Its This video game, with its exciting story and colorful graphics, is a good one for beginners. ("Its" shows possession/ownership of the story and graphics.)	**It's** It's easy to get to the next level if you concentrate. ("It's" is short for "It is.")
Your Your gaming skills are excellent. ("Your" shows possession/ownership of excellent skills.)	**You're** You're good at that game. ("You're" is short for "You are.")
Whose Whose house shall we meet at tonight? ("Whose" shows possession/ownership of the house.)	**Who's** Who's coming over after school? ("Who's" is short for " Who is.")

Verb Tense Agreement

The tense of a verb lets the reader know when the event is happening. The tense of your verbs must agree. It must be the same throughout your piece.

Present Tense:

The game system I use is excellent because it has high-quality graphics.

Past Tense:

The last gaming system I had was the best one I ever owned.

Future Tense:

One day, I will beat this game!

Editing

Because the point of an informative writing piece is to deliver data in an objective, helpful, and clear way, working with others to make sure your message has been delivered clearly is important. Give your written work to someone else, such as a classmate or teacher, to read aloud to the class or to you directly. If the presenter is reading to the class,

As you begin to revise and edit your work, having someone else read it and share his or her opinion helps you see possible revisions that you may not notice on your own.

you may want to make sure that your writing is presented anonymously. This way, listeners can listen objectively without connecting the writing back to you. With a copy of the piece in front of you, watch the audience and the reader's face while it is read. Listen for repeated words or information, or for places where the presenter stumbles or gets lost in a sentence. If you hear the words "I think" or "I feel," or similar first-person phrases, make a note of them. These phrases are subjective opinion phrases that usually don't work well in informative writing. Watch the audience for inattention or fidgety actions. These reactions could suggest that a particular moment in the story needs additional work. Notice if your transitions sound clear and if your topic is supported throughout the piece. Your ending should unite all

A SECOND LOOK

Have I incorporated spelling, grammar, and content changes into my final draft?

Does the piece deliver the information in a clear and objective way?

Is my piece full of sensory details and interesting anecdotal facts that paint a vivid picture of my topic?

Does my piece flow smoothly from point to point?

Proofreading Symbols

If your teacher or another adult has gone over your writing, he or she may have made corrections using proofreading symbols. These are used when a piece of writing is proofed for mistakes. Here is a chart of the marks you might see on your page and their meanings.

Symbol	Meaning
∧	Insert letters, words, or sentences
ℓ	Delete
∧,	Insert a comma
∨	Apostrophe or single quotation mark
∨ ∨	Double quotation marks
∼	Transpose elements (switch the order)
#	Insert a space
⌒	Close up this space
⊙	Use a period here
¶	Begin new paragraph
no ¶	No paragraph

of the information in a conclusion that reinforces your topic sentence.

If your piece is being read silently, you can take another step in receiving feedback by giving the person a short questionnaire. Once all of this information has been returned to you, reread your writing again. Now is the time to consider making last-minute changes to your final draft.

Finally, consider the following criteria. Is your title suitable? Does it grab the reader's attention? Do your opening (topic) sentence and paragraph introduce your subject in an interesting way? Is your topic sentence clear and to the point? If not, now would be a good time to edit it for length, clarity, or simplicity. Do you feel that you have presented plenty of interesting and descriptive details? Have you included at least one anecdotal fact? Make sure that your writing is organized with a distinct beginning, middle, and end. If not, you might have to reorganize your piece. Finally, does your conclusion paragraph reinforce your main points and summarize your topic clearly? Considering these criteria carefully will help you prepare your final informative piece for presentation.

chapter 6

Presenting Your Work

Whether your informational piece is a handwritten document or a computer printout, it needs to be presented neatly. If it's handwritten, make sure your paper is clean with margins and that your writing is legible. Always use black or blue ink, unless otherwise instructed. If the piece is written on the computer, use a readable font and size and check with the teacher about how to format the piece (single-spaced, double-spaced, etc.).

Now that your writing is in its final stage, focus on its presentation. If appropriate, you can enhance your writing with graphics.

For a biographical story, photos of the subject or of events in his or her life can add

ESSENTIAL STEPS

Focus on your overall presentation.

Decide if graphics would enhance the piece.

Add a bibliography if necessary.

Think of interesting ways and/or places to present your writing.

Presenting your writing in front of a group of your fellow students doesn't have to be a frightening experience. Just be yourself and keep it casual.

impact. If you are doing a report on a certain country, for example, you could use an illustration of its flag or a map.

Another component that you should include in your final informative piece is a list of the sources you used when you researched your story. This is called a bibliography, which literally means "description of books." You will most likely find much of the information needed to compile your bibliography if you used a KWL chart or a gathering grid. A bibliography is arranged in alphabetical order by the author's last name or by the title of the piece, depending on the source of the reference (see example, page 48).

Outside the Classroom

Once you've put the final touches on your informational piece, look for ways to share it with others. Ask adults to help you come up with ideas about places where your story could be submitted, or see the back matter of this book for details. Have them review Web sites where student work is shared with other writers, both professional and novices. You can brainstorm other ideas with your peers on how to publish your stories. Here are more suggestions:

Biographies

Determine an appropriate time of the year when your stories could be displayed in school.

Organize a reading around days that celebrate the theme, like a sporting season for sports figures; Mother's Day for great women in history, etc.

Organize the class stories into themes like "Sports Figures" or "Women in History."

FORMATTING A BIBLIOGRAPHY

If you are writing a paper for class, your teacher will expect your bibliography to be formatted correctly. Below is the basic way to cite your sources, but check with your teacher to make sure that this is his or her preferred style.

Books: Author or editor (last name first). Title (italicized). City where the book was published: Publisher, copyright date.

Norwich, Grace. *Daniel Radcliffe: No Ordinary Wizard*. New York: Simon & Schuster, 2008.

Magazines: Author (last name first). "Article title" (in quotation marks). Title of the magazine (italicized). Date: page number(s) of the article.

Smith, Helen. "Daniel Radcliffe: The Untold Story." *People*. September 28, 2010: 26-45.

Encyclopedias: Author (if available). "Article title" (in quotation marks). Title of the encyclopedia (italicized). Edition or version. Type other than book (CD-ROM, diskette, Web site, etc.). Date published. Available URL (address).

Schreiber, Barbara A. "Daniel Radcliffe." *Encyclopedia Britannica*. Encyclopedia Britannica Online. Dececember 17, 2010. http://www.britannica.com/EBchecked/topic/1378521/Daniel-Radcliffe.

Internet: Author (if available). "Article title" (in quotation marks). Source title (italicized). Date published. Date found. Available URL (address).

Chiu, David. "Daniel Radcliffe Wows in First Broadway Performance." People Online. 2008. Retrieved December 15, 2010. Available http://www.people.com/people/article/0,,20224037,00.html.

Interviews: Person interviewed. Type of interview. Date.

Radcliffe, Daniel. Personal interview. December 17, 2010.

Expository (or How-To) Writing

Put together a guide based on the how-to topics that have been written about, then organize it in an easy-to-use manner.

Bring in the creations that have been explained in the expository pieces and hold a show-and-tell. For example, if you've written a cookie recipe, bring in the cookies.

Informative or Personal Essays

Ask an adult to help you find a pen pal in another country to whom you can send your personal informative essay. Then ask that person to send you a similar essay in return.

Consider submitting your piece to your school newspaper, yearbook, or magazine.

Classroom Report

If your topic is the history of your school, organize a reading on the school steps or in the library, auditorium, or cafeteria.

Elaborate on your report and look deeper into the subject by finding videos, documentaries, music, art, or other works that reflect the topic, and then share them with others.

Informative writing requires a commitment to doing thorough research. Paying attention to good grammar, accurate spelling, and smooth transitions is just the beginning. Reading newspapers will help you develop a sense of how writers use facts, and not opinions, to tell their stories. Above all, listen to your instincts first, and correct your writing later. Getting your thoughts down in stages will help you develop a distinctive writer's voice. Always proofread your writing for grammatical, factual, and spelling errors. Finally, share your writing with others for constructive feedback. Before long, you'll know how to approach any type of informative writing with ease.

chapter 7
Taking Your Writing Online

Another great way to get your informative writing out there is to hit the Internet and all of the sites it has to offer to an up-and-coming author.

Wikihow

One place to start your online informative writing career is on the Web site Wikihow, a site where authors can write how-to articles that can be shared with readers. All you have to do is sign up and submit an article idea for approval. Once it's approved, you can get started researching and begin to write about your topic. When you're done, Wikihow even offers a how-to article on how to fact-check your article thoroughly so that you can make sure it's done right.

ESSENTIAL STEPS

Find quality resources online.

Seek out a Web site where you can share your work.

The best part is that you can write about almost any topic, from how to build model airplanes to how to make minor repairs to real airplanes. What's your area of expertise? You can write about it on Wikihow.

Forums and Message Boards

There are Web sites out there for almost every topic. And most of them are outfitted with places for readers to comment or join the discussion forum. Internet users often turn to Web site forums for advice, help, or discussions. If you're passionate or knowledgeable about a subject, why not join in? You never know when you might help people out with a bit of information they didn't have before.

However, keep in mind that a lot of people use these same forums to spout negative or hateful things that may not even have anything to do with the discussion. People who do that are referred to as "trolls." If you come across a troll on the discussion boards, it's best to just ignore that user. Trolls love nothing more than to get into an argument with a well-intentioned user or create general disruption to the discussion at hand. When an argument results from this kind of disturbance it is called flaming. People who deliberately create arguments are called "flamers," and they are on almost every discussion board on the Internet. It is best to not try to jump into any discussion like this, so if you see this occurring, walk away until the argument dies down.

YouTube

New videos go up on the video-sharing Web site YouTube every day. Some of them are placed there to provide helpful information to viewers. Do you want to know how to solve a Rubik's Cube? Or learn to moonwalk like Michael Jackson? You can find out how to do these things, and thousands more, on YouTube.

Do you have a special piece of knowledge that you think could benefit others? Why not make a YouTube video providing users with a step-by-step tutorial that they can follow while watching you on the screen? But no one just starts filming an informative video without writing a script beforehand, so sit down and write out what you want to say first.

Facebook

Have something informative to say? Facebook provides a place where you can say it. By creating a note, you can get your thoughts out there and even share them with your friends and invite them to share your note with others. But just as with anything you write online, make sure that what you're saying is accurate and fact-checked thoroughly.

The Internet is a great place to find good topic ideas, do some research, find tips on writing, or even post some of your writing.

Staying Safe on the Internet

If you decide to explore doing some informative writing online, make sure to keep your personal safety in mind.

If you cannot see the people to whom you are speaking in a forum or online discussion, do not trust their word about who they are. Some people use the Internet to gain the trust of others with the motive of doing them harm or gathering personal information to use for identity theft. So, be careful and trust your instincts. If someone makes you feel uncomfortable or says anything inappropriate, report that individual to that site's Webmaster.

Now, get out there and write!

GLOSSARY

adjective Word that describes a noun or pronoun.

adverb Word that describes a verb, adjective, or other adverb.

anecdote A short, entertaining account of an event.

bibliography A list of the books, articles, etc., that were used by an author while writing a piece.

biography An account of a person's life given by another.

brainstorming Collecting ideas by talking openly and writing down all the possibilities; prewriting.

chronological Arranged in the order events took place.

complex sentence A sentence formed by one independent clause and one or more dependent clauses.

compound sentence A sentence formed by joining clauses with a coordinate conjunction or a semicolon.

conjunction A word used to connect individual words or groups of words.

contraction The shortened form of a word or phrase, joined by an apostrophe.

declarative sentence A sentence that makes a strong statement.

dependent clause A clause that cannot stand on its own and depends on the rest of a sentence to make sense.

diagram A plan or drawing that explains the different elements of an idea.

essay A piece of writing in which a single topic is presented, explained, and described in an interesting way.

expository A type of writing that gives information or explains something.

feedback Information about a presented piece.

first draft The first writing of a piece without worrying about mistakes.

font A style of type for printing.

format Style or manner of a piece of writing.

independent clause A clause that expresses a complete thought and can stand alone as a sentence.

Internet Short for "interconnected networks." A place to search for information from sources all over the world.

interview A conversation between two people wherein one person asks questions of the other to gain knowledge about a subject.

margin The edge, border, or plain space around a page.

nonfiction Stories that are true.

objective To be without bias or prejudice.

paragraph A passage of writing marked by the indentation of the first sentence.

phrase A group of related words that do not express a complete thought.

plagiarism The taking of ideas, writing, etc., from another and passing them off as one's own.

proofreading Checking a final copy for any errors.

punctuation Grammatical marks used in writing.

report Account given or opinion expressed about a particular topic.

sensory details Details that use the five senses to enhance a written description.

subject The topic of a writing piece.

subjective Reflecting the feeling of a person; personal.

subtitle Explanatory phrase that supports the main title.

synonym A word that has the same meaning as another word.

thesaurus A book similar to a dictionary that offers synonyms.

topic sentence A sentence that describes what a piece of writing will be about.

transition A word or words that tie two ideas together smoothly.

verb A word that shows action or links the subject to another word in a sentence.

FOR MORE INFORMATION

Betty Award

P.O. Box 1826

Oak Park, IL 60304

Web site: http://www.thebettyaward.com
A writing contest for kids from ages eight to twelve.

National Council of Teachers of English (NCTE)

Achievement Awards in Writing

1111 Kenyon Road

Urbana, IL 61801

(217) 328-3870

Web site: http://www.ncte.org
A council of teachers devoted to improving the teaching and learning of English and the language arts at all levels of education.

Scholastic Art and Writing Awards

557 Broadway

New York, NY 10012

Web site: http://www.artandwriting.org

A writing and art contest sponsored by Scholastic, Inc.

Publishing and Posting

Merlyn's Pen

11 South Angell Street, Suite 301

Providence, RI 02906

e-mail: merlyn@merlynspen.org

Web site: http://www.merlynspen.org

Teen Ink

P.O. Box 30

Newton, MA 02461

e-mail: submissions@teenink.com

Web site: http://www.teenink.com

Skipping Stones

P.O. Box 3939

Eugene, OR 97403

(541) 342-4956

e-mail: editor@skippingstones.org

Web site: http://www.skippingstones.org

Web Sites

Due to the changing nature of Internet links, Rosen Publishing has developed an online list of Web sites related to the subject of this book. This site is updated regularly. Please use this link to access the list:

http://www.rosenlinks.com/wlp/wti

FOR FURTHER READING

Anderson, Jeff. *Everyday Editing*. Portland, ME:
Stenhouse Publishers, 2007.

Brewer, Robert Lee. *2010 Writer's Market*. Cincinnati,
OH: F + W Media, 2010.

Clark, Roy Peter. *The Glamour of Grammar: A Guide
to the Magic and Mystery of Practical English*. New
York, NY: Little Brown, 2010.

Clark, Roy Peter. *Writing Tools: 50 Essential Strategies
for Every Writer*. New York, NY: Little, Brown, 2008.

Goldberg, Natalie. *Old Friend from Far Away: The
Practice of Writing Memoir*. New York, NY: Simon &
Schuster, 2009.

Goldberg, Natalie. *Writing Down the Bones: Freeing
the Writer Within*. Boston, MA: Shambhala
Publications, 2005.

Levine, Gail Carson. *Writing Magic: Creating Stories
That Fly*. New York, NY: HarperCollins, 2006.

Strausser, Jeffrey. *Painless Writing*. Hauppage, NY:
Barron's, 2009.

Strunk, William, and E.B. White. *The Elements of
Style*. New York, NY: Longman, 1999.

Zinsser, William. *On Writing Well: The Classic
Guide to Writing Nonfiction*. New York, NY:
HarperCollins, 2006.

INDEX